BESTIARY OF CORONA ANIMALS

NIEKOLAAS JOHANNES LEKKERKERK

A Bat and a Civet Cat Sat on a Branch Reflecting on Existence
Or Meanwhile at the Huanan Seafood Market

"Are you the intermediate host?" Pangolin asked the Bat. "I am urgently looking for the intermediate host to conduct an interview about the SARS-CoV-2 pandemic."

"The intermediate host?!" exclaimed the Bat. "I am *in* the world, but I am certainly not *of* it."

"What do you mean?"

"I mean to say, I may be considered a viral metaphor these days, but let's not jump to conclusions, not just yet. Innocent until proven guilty, and even then, I am in and of myself, you understand, not a mere interlinking vessel within a geopolitical clusterfuck."

"Personally, I would gladly concur, but there are voices, even among our kind—you know how polarized we can be these days—claiming that you carried the virus, induced it even, that you are the host body this time, just as you have been so many times before."

"Humanoid scientists remain uncertain, as always... Maybe you should ask my intestines?" the bat responded with an exasperated sigh.

"But you admit that you are implicated in the viral metaphor?"

"Fine, if you insist, but I implore you to see reason! Let me explain: it all started last year on the seventeenth of November, when a man went to a seafood market, a so-called wet market—though there were also livestock on sale, as well as wolf pups, civet cats, peacocks, otters, camels even...I could go on—and bought himself a bowl of fresh clam chowder."[1]

"Not bat soup?"

"I was not *in* the soup at the time. In any case, let's keep names out of it. It's not important who that man was. He is dead, while I am alive.[2] There is a small possibility that I unintentionally sneezed onto his clams, as I am allergic to seafood. Anyway, it's not kosher to begin with."

"I can relate," interjected the Civet Cat. "'Relational asthmatics,' as they used to say! One minute you're accidentally sneezing onto a shared meal, and the next you're in the middle of the square being chopped up and divided into equal parcels, to be sold and distributed to the highest bidder first, and so on until the last. The whole rotten business goes on and on and on, and if you are dead they move onto your offspring. You're lucky you even survived to tell the story, batty! Consider the Lobster—poor, poor fellow..."[3]

The Pangolin cut in: "You've had a close relationship with Bat since the 2002 SARS outbreak. Since you're here, Civet Cat, do you think that Bat facilitated the virus's fateful leap from animals to humans?"

"That's a leading question, Pangolin reporter! The certainty you're looking for is just as fictitious as your preconceived binary between humans and animals. You're bifurcating!"

"As a news reporter, it is my duty to trace the virus to its original reservoir—which is likely a bat," said Pangolin. "Potentially, there may be a further intermediate host, another mammal species that's more widely traded in this corridor of China."

"I am sorry to say this, Pangolin, but your instincts do not strike me as fully operational. This seafood market may be a vital piece in the puzzle, but there's currently not enough evidence to categorically pinpoint the exact time, place, and species of transmission, let alone to frame Bat as the main culprit in this chain of events. You came here expecting to find Ground Zero, but you ended up with Bat and me in this deserted 'wet' market square."

Pangolin: "May I inquire, then, whether you agree with the increasingly popular notion that the virus was resting peacefully until we colonized its space, forcing an intrusion that allowed the virus to flourish in the first place?"

Civet Cat and Bat, in unison: "Who is the 'we' you're describing?"

"I have concluded that the novel coronavirus may be nature's 'revenge' on both humans and non-humans, and since we are nature, 'we are the virus.'[4] I share the belief that we are collectively and equally responsible for environmental degradation. Furthermore, the conflation of animality and humanity with the novel coronavirus, which is now replicating and spreading uncontrollably, brings up the thorny concepts of overpopulation and resource scarcity that I want to underscore."[5]

Civet Cat: "Pangolin, this is very premature thinking, and I suggest you stop spewing such eco-fascist drivel immediately. To think that this virus is Earth's vaccine...come on! That argument derives from a logic I cannot and will not follow. The virus is indifferent to these imposed binaries of yours. I have a piece of advice for you—call it a figuration. While quarantining in my cage, I subscribed to an online series of video lectures called *Four Rooms*. I know what you're thinking—'it's a luxury to have four rooms'—but one point of particular interest to me was made by Elizabeth A. Povinelli. From her book *Geontologies*, I gathered the following: 'The virus is the figure for that which seeks to disrupt the current arrangements of life and nonlife, by claiming that it is a difference that makes no difference *not because* all is alive, vital, and potent, nor because all is inert, replicative, unmoving, inert, dormant, and endurant. Because the division of life and nonlife does not define or contain the virus, it can use and ignore this division for the sole purpose of diverting the energies of arrangements of existence in order to extend itself. The virus copies, duplicates, and lies dormant even as it continually adjusts to, experiments with, and tests its circumstances. It confuses and levels the difference between life and nonlife while carefully taking advantage of the minutest aspects of their differentiation.'"[6]

Pangolin: "So you think viruses are larger than life, so to speak?"

"They are part and parcel of life's fabric. Viruses are the 'threads' of life's spider web: the more threads are cut, the greater the potential for danger to be inflicted.[7] We evolve together with 'our' viruses. Whereas viruses have existed since time immemorial, their current resurgence has more to do with the colonization and intensified usage of lands that were previously inhabited only by us 'wild' animals. Yet for me, humans are where the wild things are and where wild things happen: they shift the balance of our environment with their intimidating activities. I mean, Bat and I are considered delicacies, while you, Pangolin, are poached for your meat and scales, to be used in traditional medicine to cure whatever human ailment. Rather than rights-bearing subjects, we are no more than commodities, assets,

1 Sentence modeled after text from Robert Filliou's "Whispered History of Art," recorded in New York in 1977.
2 Ibid.
3 David Foster Wallace's essay "Consider the Lobster" concerns the ethics of boiling a creature alive in order to enhance consumer pleasure, and includes a discussion of the lobster's sensory neurons. David Foster Wallace, "Consider the Lobster," in *Consider the Lobster – And Other* Essays (New York: Little, Brown and Company and Time Warner Book Group, 2005), 235–55.
4 Tom (@tomschulz), "Wow... Earth is recovering," Twitter message, March 17, 2020, https://twitter.com/ThomasSchulz/status/1239935787619115012.
5 Jennifer Johnson, "We are not the virus," *Verso* (27 March 2020), https://www.versobooks.com/blogs/4622-we-are-not-the-virus.
6 Elizabeth A. Povinelli, *Geontologies: A Requiem to Late Liberalism* (Durham: Duke University Press, 2016), 18–19.
7 Sanne Bloemink, "Het is niet de schuld van de vleesmuis," *De Groene Amsterdammer*, no. 15 (April 2020).

investments, nourishment, goods in trade—but *animals*? The whole process of zoonosis and species jump seems to begin there, informing a direct correlation and chain of causality between human objectification of the world, their extractivist practices, the current climate regime and the outbreak of the novel coronavirus pandemic...but I should stop there. I heard that Cow and Chicken have more to say on this point."

Bat starts humming a song: "If you leave me now, you'll take away the biggest part of me? ...I just want you to stay... How could we let it slip away? ...We've come too far to leave it all behind...How could we end it all this way?"[8]

8 Sentence modeled on text from the hit ballad "If You Leave Me Now" by American rock group Chicago, released as a single in 1976.

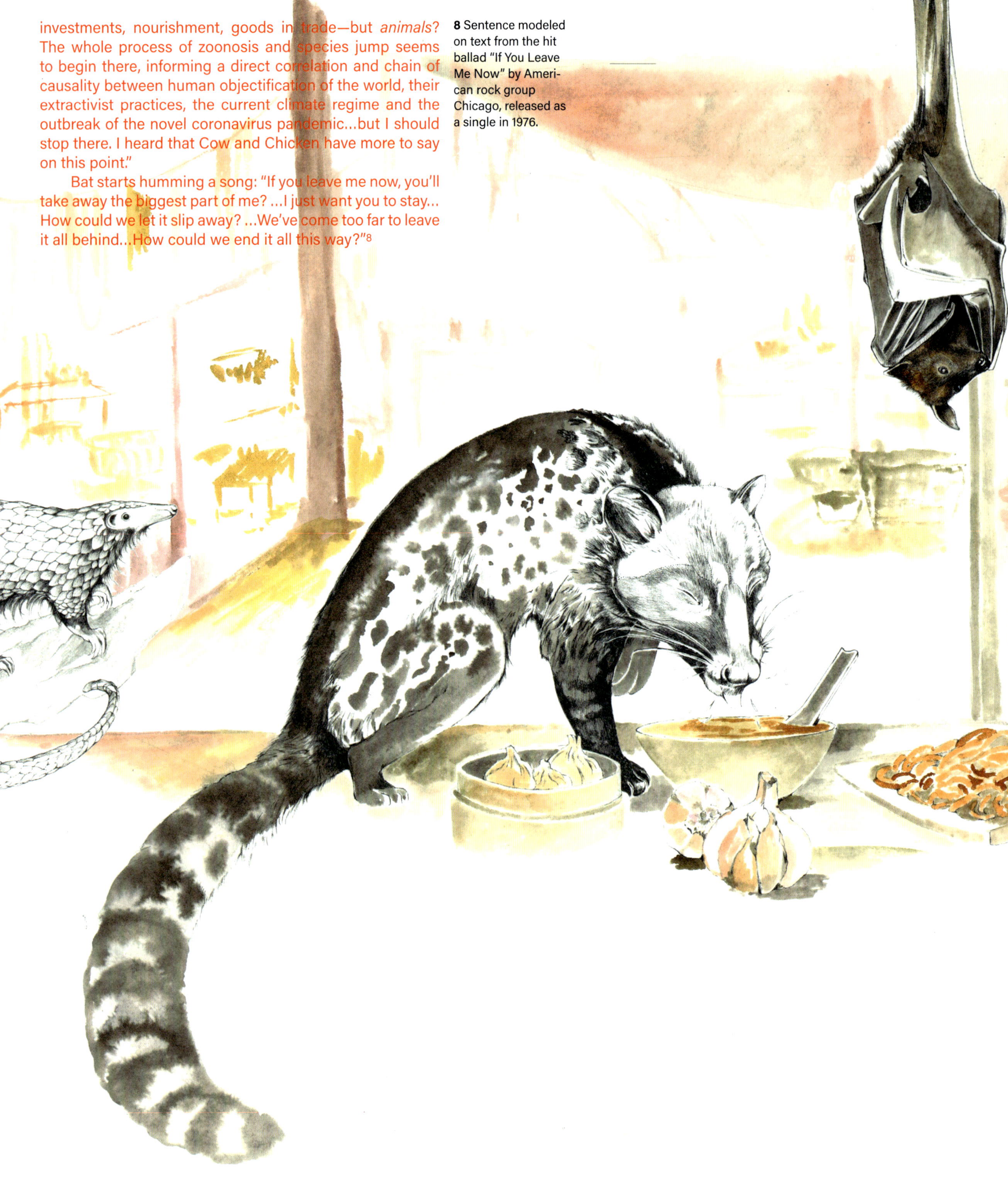

Never Go to the Carnival Naked

Or Meanwhile in the Land of Monoculture with Cow and Chicken

We are Cow and Chicken. You could replace us with pigs, goats, horses, soy, and palm oil plantations even: it kind of matters but it kind of doesn't. We are not single specimens of different kinds; we are legion. We are a statistic. We are multiplications of one, quantified as our net weight in protein, indexed along the vectors of advanced capitalism. Valorizing, calorizing. Our economy and ecology have become sites for algorithms of progress-as-expansion.[9] We are consumable three-dimensional assets in styrofoam trays, resting on absorbent pads that collect the excretions of our blood and the water injected into our bodies—another technique devised under capitalism to achieve alienation, or in this case abstraction, obscuring the mutilation of our natural forms, suppressing your empathy, turning us into resources for investment and purchase. Or, in the words of Donna Haraway, our history coincides with "the relentless hormonal growth promotion of the next molecular generations, which is integral to the destruction of ecosystems, transformation of human and animal labor, mutilation of multispecies souls, spread of epidemics, affinity for monocrop corn, and cross-species heartbreak of feedlot cattle industries."[10]

Where do we live now and how did we end up here? We inhabit facilities that bear no resemblance to farms. We are trapped in industrial complexes that are also frameworks for humans' insatiable urge towards progress. We live in standardized, self-contained units for uniform growth, designed and calibrated (not unlike our cross-bred genome) to keep external foreign agents, including bacteria and viruses, at a safe distance. When we contract a disease, "we" literally die as members of species in which we are all identical. Our facilities are modeled on plans for plantation-style alienation.[11] We live according to a unified coordination of time: welcome to the land of monoculture!

This is where we ended up, and all the while, fossil-burning man has been making new fossils as rapidly as possible in the orgies of the Anthropocene and Capitalocene.[12] As Anna Tsing mentions, "no place in the world is untouched by that global political economy built from the postwar development apparatus."[13] "There is a chemical conjunction between the history of fertilizers and the history of war and technological culture," to paraphrase Jussi Parikka, and "industrialization becomes a point of synchronization between the various lineages of cultural techniques. In the scientific age, the agricultural metaphor of 'culturing' is part of the development of chemical means of manipulation of the soil."[14] That history includes our story: before us, there was a forest, a tropical rainforest in the Amazon. We live today on the soil where indigenous communities once dwelled, only to be displaced and slaughtered by political regimes working hand-in-hand with mercenary corporations engaged in fossil fuel extraction, illegal or fraudulently-sanctioned logging, or mining for gold, uranium, coal, and rare earth minerals. In place of the original communities eviscerated by deforestation or agriculture, there arose a second layer—the monocrop cultivation and livestock bio-industrial complex in which we live to this day. Genocide and ecocide are simply two sides of the same coin in such struggles for land sovereignty.[15] We do not want to jump to conclusions, but we are running out of time.

What is our relation to the novel coronavirus? We belong to different pictures, with different scales and reaches. "Growing genetic monocultures of domestic animals discourages any immunity firebreaks from developing to slow down transmission. Larger population size and density facilitate greater rates of transmission. Crowded conditions depress immune responses. High throughput, essential to any industrial production, provides a continually renewed supply of 'susceptibles,' the fuel for the evolution of virulence."[16] We are the millions of reservoirs and pathways of zoonoses, the infectious diseases transmitted from non-human animals to humans—including ebola (2013–2016 epidemic, and still ongoing), SARS (2002–2004 outbreak, with renewed interest), MERS (2012, camel flu), swine flu (2009 pandemic centered in Mexico), and especially HIV (millions of deaths since the early 20th century). First there is the virus, then the initial host—for instance, the bat (whose infection is asymptomatic)—then the species jump, bringing us to the present stage of the transmission host, with moderate to severe symptoms, ending with the spillover host, the human, with severe infection and high mortality rates. These viral species jumps and spillovers often occur in the process of catching, selling, and consuming bats, civet cats, camels, pigs, or chimpanzees.

The radical eradication of "relatively untouched" environments driven by humans disturbs the balance of ecologies, involving different intra-active soil compositions and lifeforms, from animals and fungi to bacteria and plants. These organisms contain and transport different microbes, and when the host species are endangered through the destruction of their living environments (for instance, through deforestation), parasites such as viruses are uprooted and subsequently seek, adapt, and select for new host bodies.[17] Since humans are not all that sparse in number nor stationary in location, viruses can count their blessings. Human encounters with bats, cockroaches, rats, pigeons, mice, and mosquitos—all of the "usual [vermin] suspects" in these environments—bring additional windfalls, as these species have evolved to invest their energy and development mainly in reproduction, rather than more elaborate immune systems. They carry more pathogens and are capable of surviving in environments disturbed by humans. The faster that humans invade environments with high biodiversity, such as tropical rainforests, the more these "quick-on-their-[reproductive]-feet" species will displace more fragile organisms. The diminishing biodiversity and radical depletion of lifeforms—the consequences of extractivist practices, including mining and deforestation to make way for agriculture—are accompanied by an increase in infectious diseases that could spill over to humans.[18]
We are an ongoing multispecies genocide thrown into the insatiable abyss of natural capital. With the foresight of the negative economic impact to be inflicted by the novel coronavirus pandemic, this rupture in the real could grow so large that it would eventually gulp down wildlife and cattle; as one fund manager has written, "Virus is like a huge

9 Anna Lowenhaupt Tsing, *The Mushroom at the End of the World: On the Possibility of Life in Capitalist Ruins* (Princeton and Oxford: Princeton University Press, 2015), 28.
10 Donna Haraway, *Staying with the Trouble: Making Kin in the Chthulucene* (Durham and London: Duke University Press, 2016), 109.
11 Tsing, *The Mushroom at the End of the World*, 40.
12 Haraway, *Staying with the Trouble*, 55.
13 Tsing, *The Mushroom at the End of the World*, 3.
14 Jussi Parikka, *A Geology of Media* (Minneapolis and London: University of Minnesota Press, 2015), 53.
15 Paulo Tavares, "The Political Nature of the Forest: A Botanic Archeology of Genocide," in *The Word for World is Still Forest*, ed. A. Springer, E. Turpin (Berlin: K. Verlag and Haus der Kulturen der Welt, 2017), 125–157.
16 Rob Wallace, Alex Liebman, Luis Fernando Chaces, and Rodrick Wallace, "COVID-19 and the Circuits of Capital," *Monthly Review* (April 2020).
17 Christian Walzer, "Opinion: To Reduce the Likelihood of Future Pandemics, We Need to Rethink Our Relationship with Wild Animals and Wild Places," *ensia* (April 2020), https://ensia.com/voices/covid-19-coronavirus-pandemic-wild-animals-ecosystems/.
18 Paragraph paraphrased from: Sanne Bloemink, "Het is niet de schuld van de vleesmuis," *De Groene Amsterdammer*, no. 15 (April 2020).

sinkhole in the global economy. No one...knows how big/deep it is. And every day world is in lockdown, it gets bigger and deeper. Policy makers have no clue, but they have to do something, so they have started shoveling fiscal and monetary "dirt" into hole. If hole bigger than dirt, we get deflation...If dirt bigger than hole, you get...inflation. And if, by dumb luck, dirt=hole, back to Goldilocks"—just right. The fund manager's calculation: "hole > dirt."[19]

If you ask us, we would love to become part of the process that Anna Tsing calls resurgence. "The cross-species relations that sustain complex ecosystems are renewed in the regrowing forest. Resurgence is the work of many organisms, negotiating through and across difference. Humans will sacrifice their livelihood without it."[20] However, instead of governments worldwide opting for regrowing forests, we see deniers of climate change and the coronavirus, like Brazilian president Jair Bolsonaro, supporting and investing in neocolonial practices to further excavate the most diverse ecosystems on Earth, including the Amazon. Some would even argue that we are all complicit on an individual level; as David Quammen says, everyone with a mobile phone is responsible. Every phone and laptop contains coltan, derived from a mine in the Democratic Republic of the Congo. In order to extract coltan, the rainforest is cut down, simultaneously destroying the habitat of gorillas who are already near extinction. Coltan is mined alongside the region of the tropical rainforest where bats live, amplifying the risk of species jump of pathogenic viruses. People in precarious circumstances are sent to work in the coltan mines, where they consume bushmeat from the neighbouring forest to survive. This intensified confrontation between human and non-human animals, in turn, increases the chance of a virus spreading between species.[21] But let us not deceive ourselves: both the current climate regime and viral pandemic, like previous disturbances to stable environmental and health conditions, always hit the hardest for impoverished communities living in states of urgency, in which people can only dream of having a large carbon footprint. Greater personal wealth is plainly and indisputably correlated with the acceleration of environmental and biological threats. Yes, there is a logic to be changed.[22]

19 Nick Paumgarten, "The Price of the Coronavirus Pandemic," *The New Yorker* (April 2020).
20 Anna Lowenhaupt Tsing, "A Threat to Holocene Resurgence is a Threat to Liveability," in *The Anthropology of Sustainability*, ed. M. Brightman, J. Lewis (New York: Palgrave Macmillen, 2017), 52.
21 Sanne Bloemink, "Het is niet de schuld van de vleesmuis," *De Groene Amsterdammer*, no. 15 (April 2020).
22 Leo Bottrill, "Protecting Forests is Critical to Public Health," *MapHubs* (21 March 2020), https://medium.com/maphubs/protect-primary-forests-to-break-coronavirus-supply-chains-c99f943fbc37.

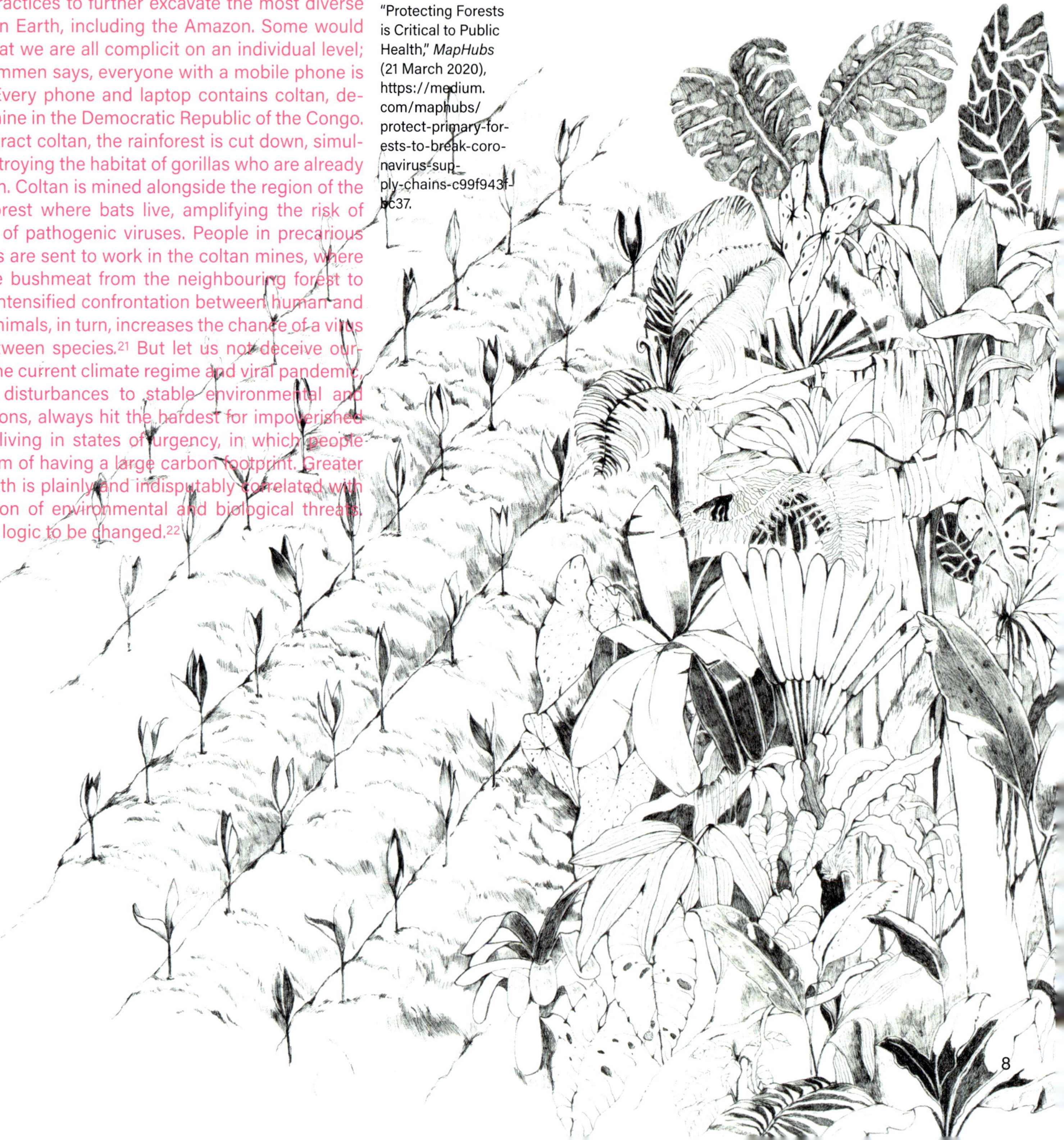

An Interview between Camel Octave and Human Hans Ulrich Obrist
Or Meanwhile in an Art World with Acute Respiratory Distress Syndrome

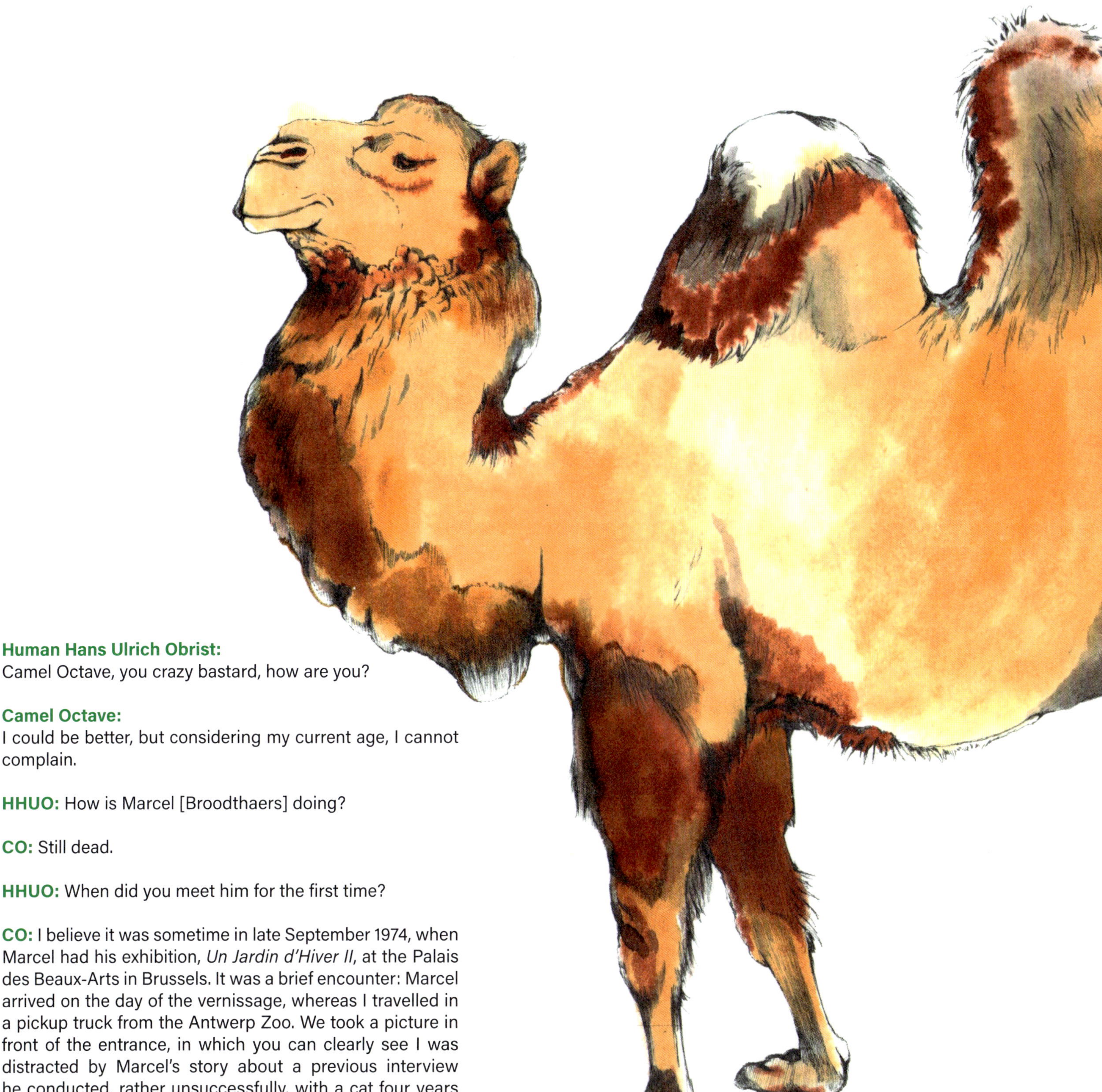

Human Hans Ulrich Obrist:
Camel Octave, you crazy bastard, how are you?

Camel Octave:
I could be better, but considering my current age, I cannot complain.

HHUO: How is Marcel [Broodthaers] doing?

CO: Still dead.

HHUO: When did you meet him for the first time?

CO: I believe it was sometime in late September 1974, when Marcel had his exhibition, *Un Jardin d'Hiver II*, at the Palais des Beaux-Arts in Brussels. It was a brief encounter: Marcel arrived on the day of the vernissage, whereas I travelled in a pickup truck from the Antwerp Zoo. We took a picture in front of the entrance, in which you can clearly see I was distracted by Marcel's story about a previous interview he conducted, rather unsuccessfully, with a cat four years earlier.

"This is not a pipe."
"This is a pipe."
"Pipe is not."

I found it hi-la-ri-ous!

After that, we—Marcel, me, two zookeepers, and the members of a recording crew—entered the venue, a process that was recorded and broadcast live on a TV monitor as part of the exhibition. It was part of the double representations Marcel was talking about at the time.

HHUO: From a dialogue between Marcel and an unspecified male interviewer, I understand the action was considered "a gesture which declares that the current situation is deeply desperate, a situation that could give the artistic act itself a cynical quality." Marcel responded, in turn, by saying that, for him, "the camel is about non-communication. The camel is animal beauty. I'd say that the rest doesn't interest me, I mean, the palm, the museum. To make things clear, 'I'd say' means that I'm not saying it. But for me the camel is beauty, and beauty as in the Baudelaire poem: 'I am beautiful, O mortals, like a dream of stone.'"[23] For Marcel, in other words, it was more about the trace of the visit than about exhibiting animals or humans, about viewing the notion of beauty at the time as something comical. What do you think about this act, in retrospect?

CO: I did not mind the exposure, really, or being part of an argument that underscored the oscillation and contrast between what is deemed exotic—me, the potted palm trees, the orientalist engravings—and what is regarded as cozily domestic. I somehow look back at that experience through a sentimental lens—a time when artists were still able to provoke a shift in signification and meaning via the displacement of aesthetic registers, in which I functioned as a signifier for the comical banality of "great beauty" in a petit bourgeois society with a colonial hangover, so to speak. Comical, yes, but the aspect of non-communication saddens me still. It is really about this incapacity of humans to be empathic towards non-human animals—their languages, politics, wellbeing—and the startling force of animal objectification. In that sense I am pleased to be able to express myself now, here in this interview with you.

At the time, the gap between nature and culture was still clearly distinct, whereas now *naturecultures* are inextricably linked, entangled, enmeshed. Broodthaers was quick to inhabit that gap, but at best, it informed a discussion around escapism and loss, not really about institutionalization—there is no stopping the institution of human supremacism and exceptionalism—or the structural inequalities and mistreatment enacted by humans towards non-human animals. Perhaps, unknowingly, Marcel connected the universe, or at least an aspect of it, with the (art) institution, if only temporarily. But what could I contribute to the institution's moral and ethical inheritance, apart from being provocative or subversive?

Let me tell you something else: after the Broodthaers act I contracted the MERS virus—causing Middle East Respiratory Syndrome—most likely from one of the many onlookers that touched me or coughed and sneezed in my proximity, after contracting the virus themselves while traveling in the Middle East. It reminds of the current situation with the coronavirus: these viruses easily disseminate through networks created by humans. Ebola traveled by car, the coronavirus by airplane.[24] You travel often, don't you?

HHUO: Did you get a proper fee, ample renumeration, reimbursement of travel costs, sojourns? What about your insurance for working on site rather than at the zoo?

CO: No, the Belgian tradition was, and to a large extent still is, not to pay anyone. However, I value vitality over finances; I was literally on the brink of death.

HHUO: You are a Bactrian Camel, right?

CO: *Camelus bactrianus*, going strong since 1758.[25]

HHUO: I thought only Dromedary Camels could contract and spread the MERS virus?

CO: We are receptive to the same pathogens.

HHUO: Any symptoms?

CO: High fever, coughing, and diarrhea, but no shortness of breath or respiratory problems—you see, at the time I was still young and in good athletic shape. In any case, I survived, but at least 640 people died. Speaking of which, how is your *Extinction as Usual Marathon* going?

HHUO: It was the *Extinction Marathon*, but that ended in 2014. Currently I am busy with the Serpentine's fiftieth anniversary.

CO: How is that going? Has it become more of a half-marathon, with the impact of the current coronavirus pandemic?

HHUO: This turning point has allowed us to pause and think: what is our role as an exhibition space, as a facility for artists and ideas, as an archive and catalyst? This has made us pledge to find new ways of thinking and acting. Ecology will be at the heart of everything that we do.[26]

CO: Which turning point, the anniversary or the coronavirus pandemic?

HHUO: The anniversary, first and foremost, but the pandemic really adds to our novel idea of "slow programming." Can we explore what might be called sustainable curation and develop new standards of practice?[27] How can we activate our institutions when they are physically closed to the public? How do you establish relationships with your publics in the time of social distancing?

CO: To me it sounds rather arbitrary to model this "turning point" on the mere givenness of an anniversary. One should always be wary of ascribing significance to numerical milestones: days, years and decades are both sloppier and infinitely more capacious than their calendrical boundaries imply, especially vis-à-vis the current climate regime and ecological breakdown. Not to say your focus is not valid, it just doesn't sound coherent if you accept that ecological degradation has already been going on for decades. Best trends forever?

HHUO: It's a slow awakening, for sure, but that's the whole point.

23 Author unknown, "Interviews with Marcel Broodthaers at The Atelier de Création Radiophonique, 1970–1975," in *Marcel Broodthaers: Collected Writings*, ed. G. Moure (Barcelona: Ediciones Polígrafa, 2012), 456.
24 Sanne Bloemink, "Het is niet de schuld van de vleesmuis," *De Groene Amsterdammer*, no. 15 (April 2020).
25 Following Linnaeus' classification in *Systems Naturae* (1735).
26 Hans Ulrich Obrist, "Ecology will be at the heart of everything we do," *The Art Newspaper*, no. 320 (February 2020).
27 Ibid.

CO: During a crisis that has killed hundreds of thousands of people, to call it an "awakening" implies that humans are disposable, that large-scale death and suffering are necessary to restore nature.

HHUO: I was referring to the ecological reality.

CO: Yes, yes. I am sorry to be frank with you, but you have logged 3,864,312 air miles, you buy a book each day, and until a few years ago everything you did was "somehow connected to velocity."[28] You are the embodiment of the art world's complicity in fossil expressionism! Do you think this new approach is credible, now, suddenly, when the world is on fire and your feedback loops have yet to come full circle?

HHUO: For years I paid into a carbon offset fund every time I flew, but this is not enough. From this year on I will follow [Gustav] Metzger's advice and reduce my flying substantially. I hope that as I reduce my travel, I can contribute by popularizing methods of exchange that are more tenable for the wellbeing of the planet. I want to put into practice some of the lessons I have learned from artists. Improving one's individual actions cannot hurt the collective effort to mitigate climate crisis, but it is only through systemic organizational change that sufficient progress can be made towards sustainable practices. Art institutions can be a tool to bridge geographies, ideas, and ways of life. When artists like Metzger can avail of their platforms, the direst problems of the world can be understood using honesty and hope.[29]

CO: How will you implement systemic organizational change in the Serpentine Galleries, to counterbalance the art world's reliance on carbon, its over-indebtedness to petro-subjectivity?[30]

HHUO: It's very important to inject experiences of slowness. I think curating exhibitions means having slow lanes—not only fast lanes.[31]

CO: Do you believe that we can infer structures of being from structures of lived experience? In other words—and worlds still—do you think that this will equip the public to aspire towards radical change on a political-governmental level? Or is it just greenwashing...

HHUO: Genau, or as my dear friend Warren Beatty once said, "I'd rather ride down the street on a camel than give what is sometimes called an 'in-depth' interview."[32]

28 Rachel Cooke, "Hans Ulrich Obrist: 'Everything I do is somehow connected to velocity,'" *The Guardian* (8 March 2015), https://www.theguardian.com/artanddesign/2015/mar/08/hans-ulrich-obrist-everything-i-do-connected-velocity-interview.
29 Hans-Ulrich Obrist, "Ecology will be at the heart of everything we do," *The Art Newspaper*, no. 320 (February 2020).
30 Term coined by Brett Bloom in *Petro-Subjectivity: De-Industrializing Our Sense of Self* (Ft. Wayne: Breakdown Break Down Press, 2015).
31 Hans Ulrich Obrist, "Hans Ulrich Obrist On The Pace of The World And the Value of Slowness," *Farnam Street*, https://fs.blog/2014/06/hans-ulrich-the-value-of-slowness/.
32 David Blum, "The Road to Ishtar," *New York Magazine*, no. 11 (March 1987), p. 38.

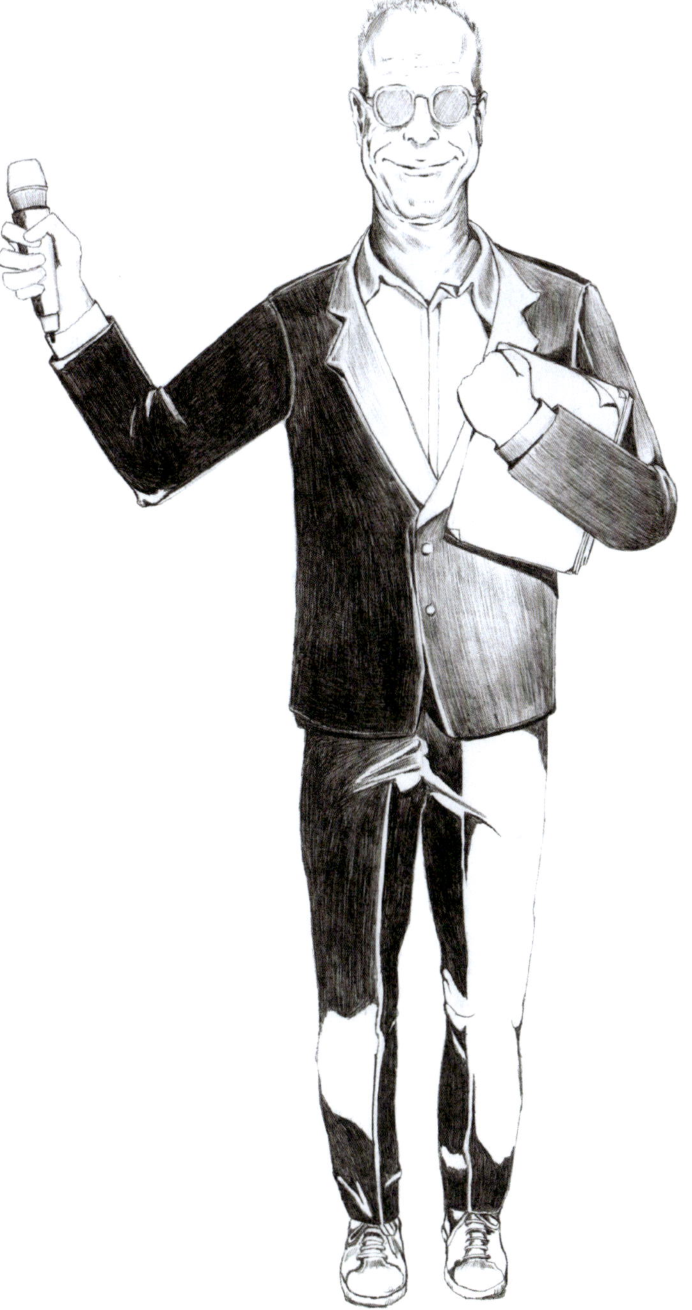

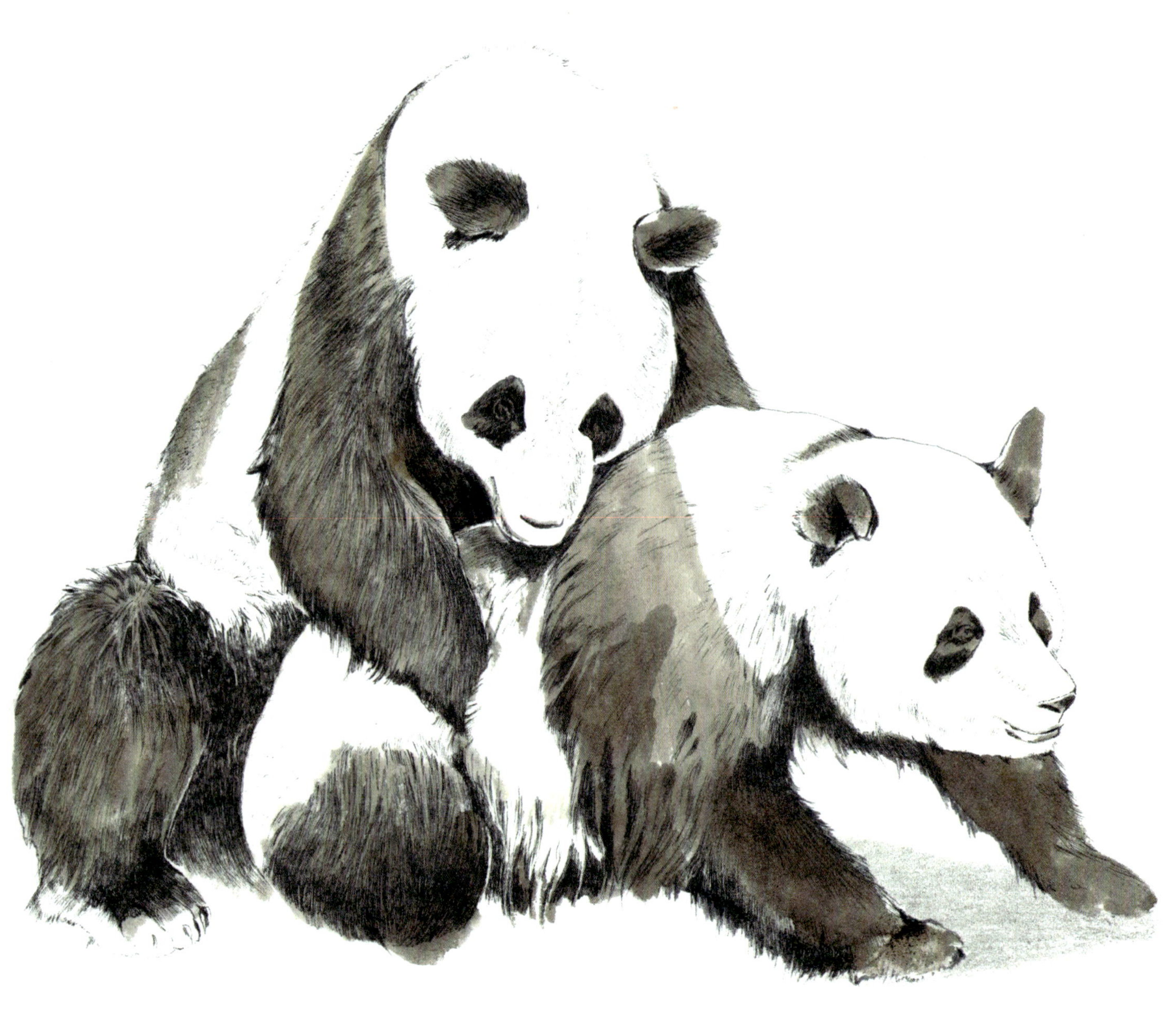

A Report to an Academy

Or Meanwhile at the Zoo with Tiger, Penguin, and Panda

Honored members of the Academy![33]

You have done me the honor of inviting me to give your Academy an account of the life I formerly led as a tiger in a public zoo.

I regret that I cannot comply with your request to the extent you desire. While you spent your days in (self-)imposed solitary confinement, The Tiger King was imprisoned, and I, Nadia, the former Malaysian tiger at the Bronx Zoo, contracted and have been gradually recovering from a respiratory indisposition caused by the public's coronation of a virus, and I must admit, the disease has proven wildly unpredictable.[34]

But to a lesser extent I can perhaps meet your demand, and indeed I do so with the greatest pleasure. The first thing I learned at the zoo was to give a handshake; a handshake betokens frankness; well, today no physical interaction—let alone handshakes—are permitted, and the human public resides elsewhere, barred from this zoo.

In order to distract us from the melancholic sentiments that may creep up occasionally during these unsettling times, we have metaphorically opened the gates of our cages and developed special programs and activities for both the externalized public and the inhabitants of this zoo to enjoy. #socialsolidarity

To use a metaphor, we have turned the frames of our zoo inside-out. Where the building is normally divided—the public in one half, the penguins in the other—we have taken the penguins on a guided tour of the zoo habitats, in this case the Amazon-themed area. They enjoyed watching the exotic fish swimming in the glass-fronted tank and visiting the aquarium's rotunda. The public, in turn, enjoyed watching the live broadcast on Facebook. We were all quite delighted.[35]

One rumor reached us that two pandas successfully mated this Monday, after a dry period of ten years. Honored members, I hear you thinking, "This is simply Darwinism doing its work," but this deed of overcoming historically low libidos has been a cause for celebration in the world of animal conservation. The act was completed after a period of foreplay involving typical panda courtship, including leaving scent markings around the habitat and playing with water. Staff members stood by and captured some slightly risqué photographs of the romantic deed. My report concludes that the pandas finally had some privacy after the zoo closed its gates to the public due to the outbreak of the coronavirus.[36]

Honored members, let me conclude this report of my findings. I have gathered that just as the soil counterbalances carbon dioxide produced by plants, normal behavior makes up for the constructedness, the artificiality of our surroundings. I understand normal to mean not looking deeper than a certain level.[37] *It implies not looking deeper into the scripts, protocols and objectivist forms of rationality that have coded the institution in which I am exhibited today. Not looking deeper into the anthropomorphisms, the representations, the knowledges imposed and imparted on my being, the display and* mise-en-scène *of my "natural habitat," reconstructed as a configured, conditioned and domesticated type of spatiotemporality.*

That progress of mine! How the rays of knowledge penetrated from all sides into my awakening brain! I do not deny it: I found it exhilarating. But I must also confess: I did not overestimate it, not even then, much less now. With an effort which up till now has never been repeated I managed to reach the cultural level of an average European. In itself that might be nothing to speak of, but it is something insofar as it has helped me out of my cage and opened a special way out for me, the way of humanity. There is an excellent idiom: to fight one's way through the thick of things; that is what I have done, I have fought through the thick of things. There was nothing else for me to do, provided always that freedom was not to be my choice.

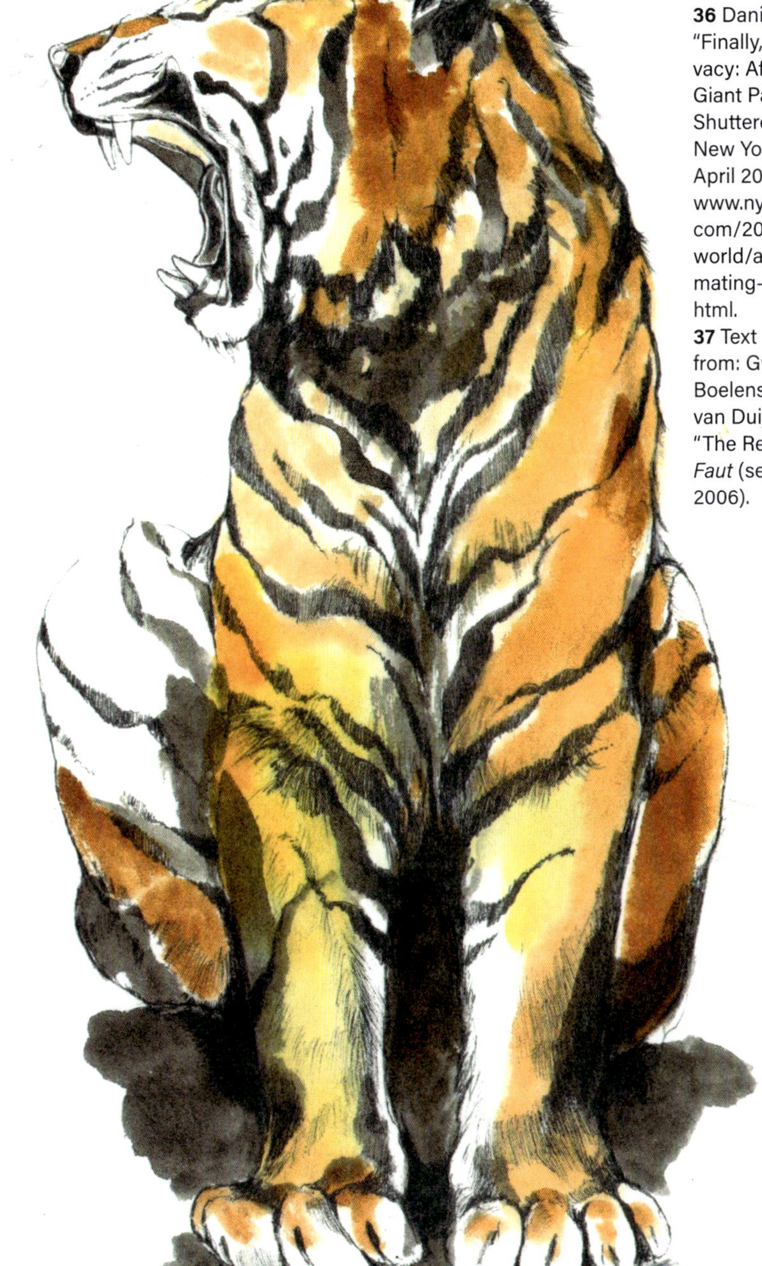

33 This section cites from and is modeled after: Franz Kafka, "A Report to an Academy," in *The Complete Short Stories*, ed. N.N. Glatzer (London: Vintage, The Random House Group Limited, 2005), 250–258.

34 Kate Knibbs, "The Real Reason Veterinarians Gave a Tiger a Covid-19 Test," *Wired* (12 April 2020), https://www.wired.com/story/tiger-coronavirus-bronx-zoo/.

35 Jimmy McCloskey, "Penguins roam free after aquarium is closed by coronavirus," *Metro* (17 March 2020), https://metro.co.uk/2020/03/17/penguins-get-guided-tour-aquarium-live-coronavirus-closure-12414210/.

36 Daniel Victor, "Finally, Some Privacy: After 10 Years, Giant Pandas Mate in Shuttered Zoo," The New York Times (7 April 2020), https://www.nytimes.com/2020/04/07/world/asia/panda-mating-hong-kong.html.

37 Text paraphrased from: Gwenneth Boelens and Nickel van Duijvenboden, "The Retained," in *Il Faut* (self-published, 2006).

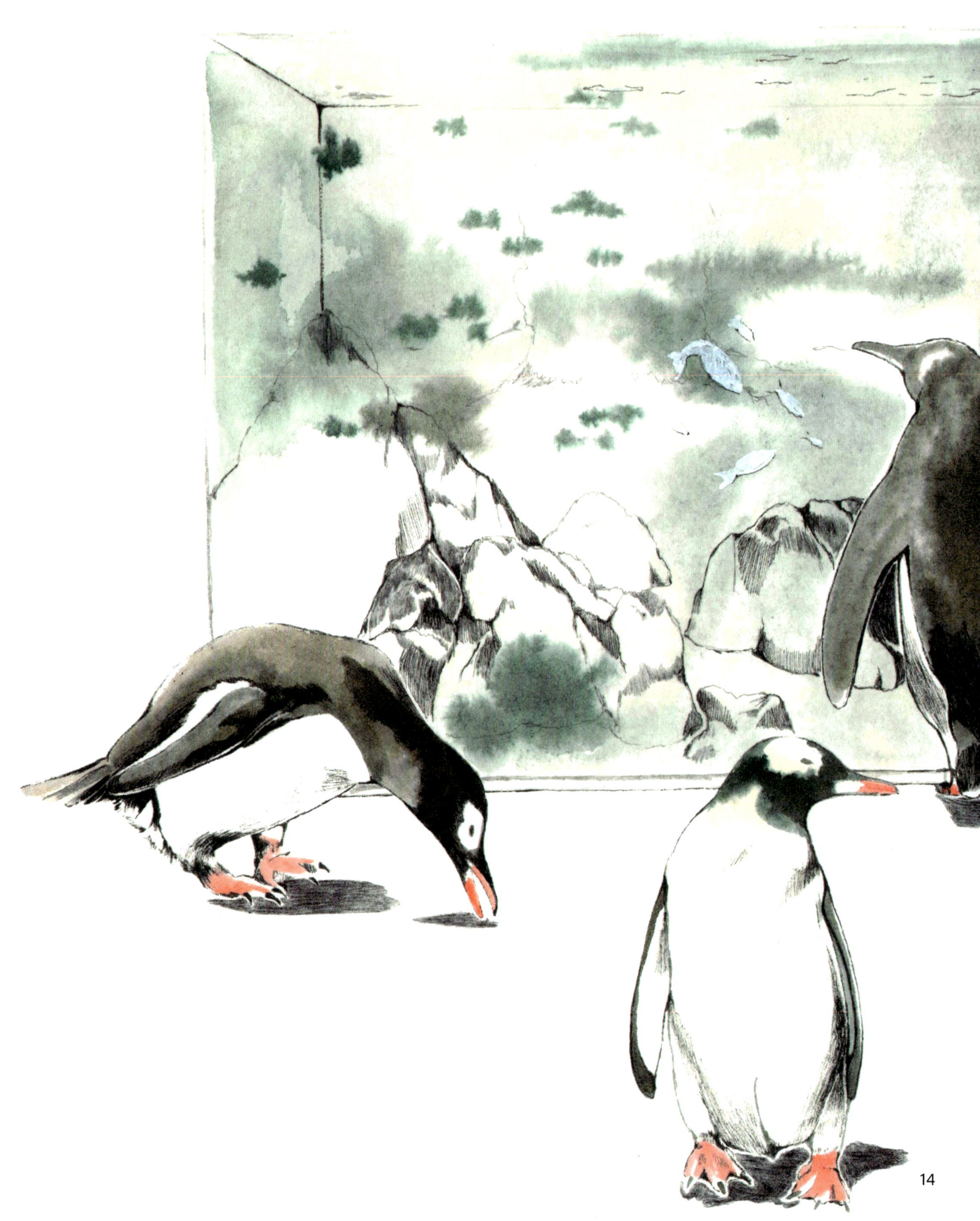

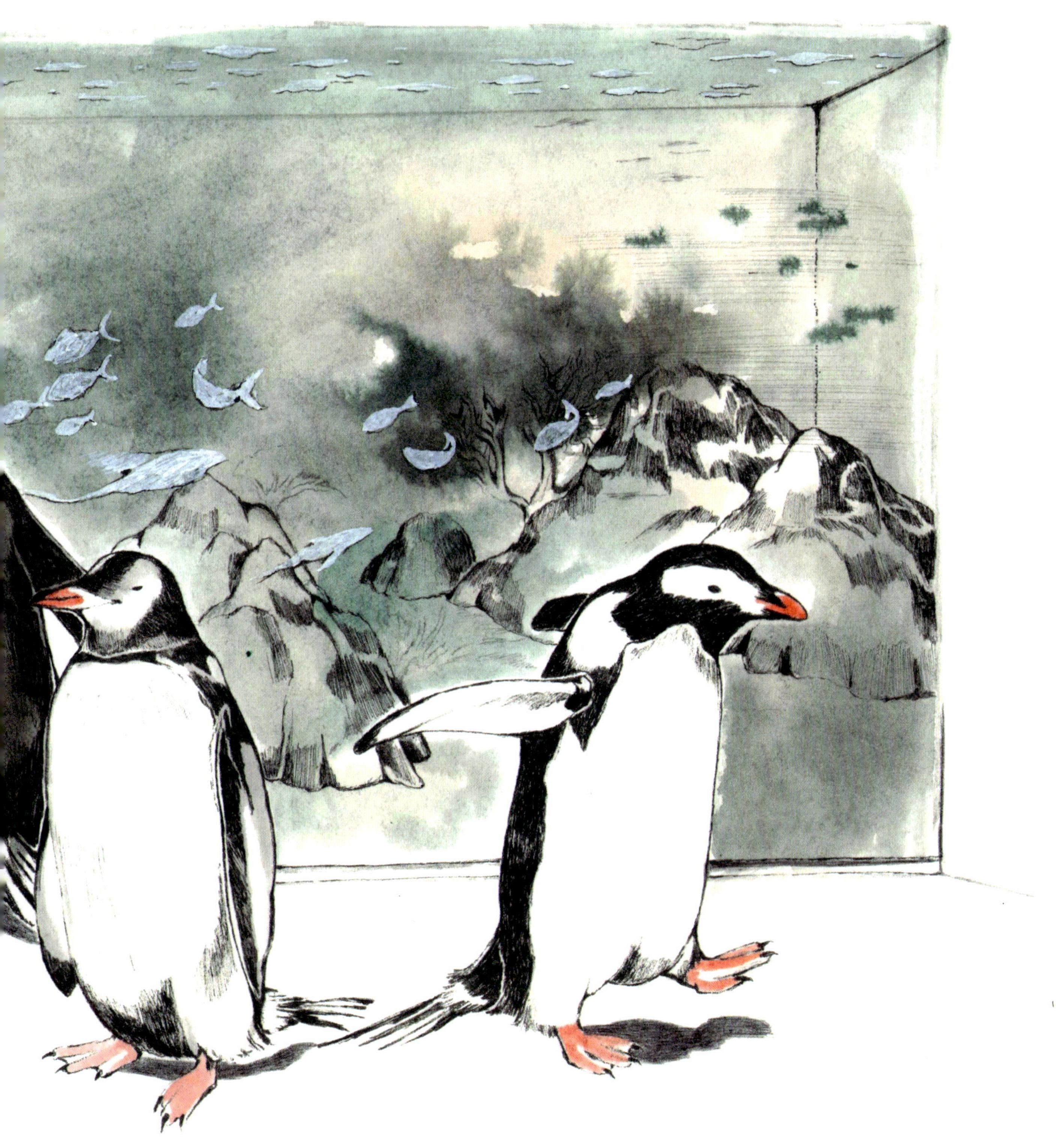

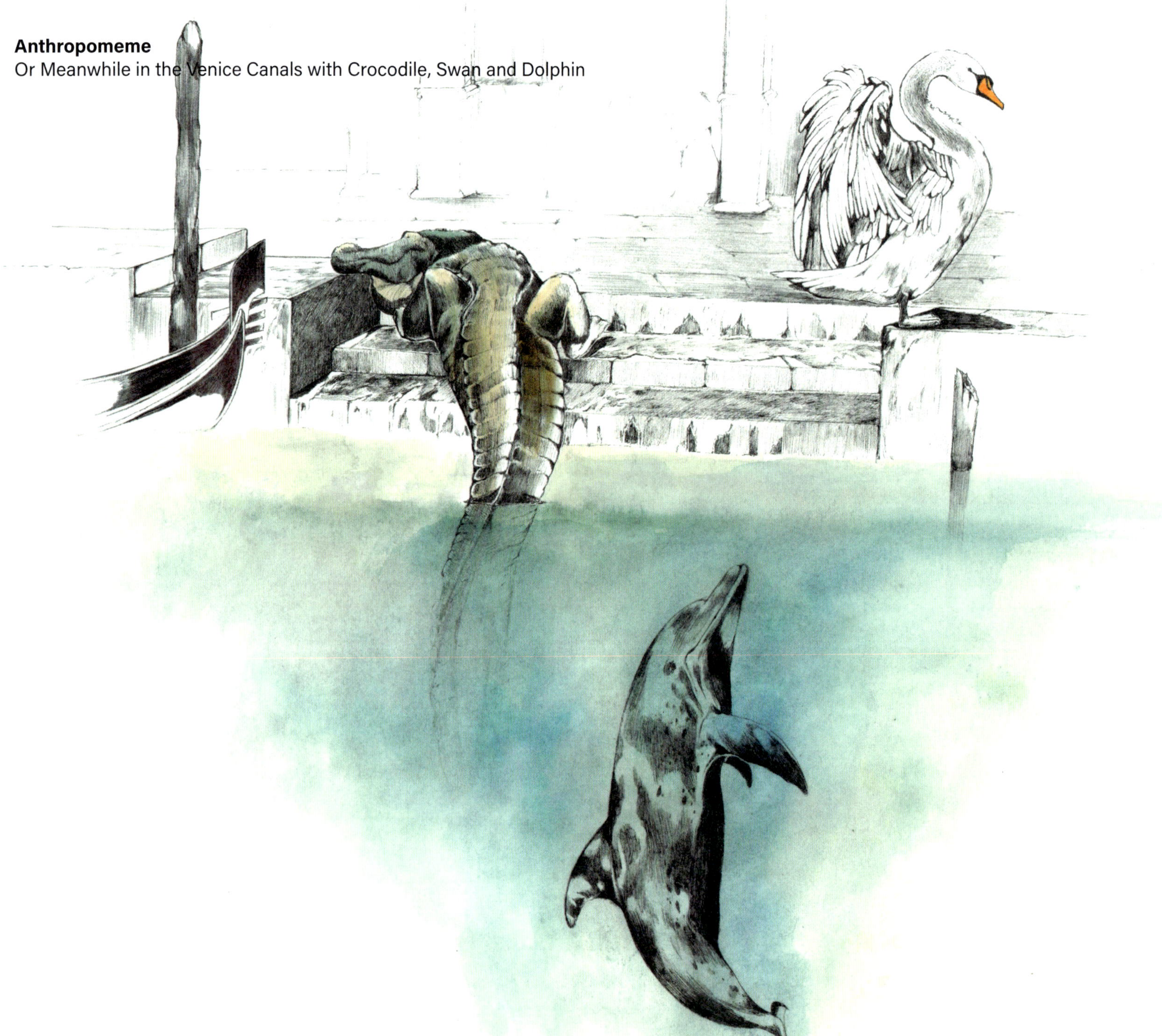

"Anthropocene, Undocene, Manthropocene, Smanthropocene, Endcene, Smog-o-machine, Plasticene, Psychozooikon, Psychozoiocene, Northropocene, Connectozoic, Chthulhucene, Anthropo-not-scene, Hypocricene, Plantationocene, Capitalocene, Anthrobscene, Androcene, Schnubeleduldidlocene, Anthro-what-not-scene, Misanthropocene, Prokaryocene, Oops-a-daisy-cene—what do you think, Swan, any of them to your liking?"

Swan: "Personally, I am fond of Capitalocene. Do you remember the viral image of two people engulfed by the Venice floods while trying to keep their Louis Vuitton bags above the water? It's often captioned with the quote usually attributed to Fredric Jameson: 'It is easier to imagine the end of the world than the end of capitalism.' I find it particularly apt for thinking about the anthropos and their collective death drive."

"That *is* a particularly good one, I agree, but don't you think the 'human-capital-world' equation is a massive generalization? I mean, what about us animals, for a start?"

"Well, Dolphin, I suppose the same goes for most of these 'scenes': they are based on a false universal conception of 'humanity,' this singular kind of 'species act' that is humanity—not human—or what art historian T.J. Demos would call 'human exceptionalism.'[38] On the other wing I was reminded of evolutionary theorist and biologist Lynn Margulis and her writing about life producing its own environment, the idea that living forms are not found *in* an environment, but that they (including humans) have ended up *making* it. We and our cells, we all evolve together.[39] In that sense the Capitalocene is a striking figure, as I suppose that what we are witnessing—the ecological breakdown of the environment and the degradation of biodiversity and the Earth's biofilm—is being led by the objectifying impetus of humanity. Instead of thinking and speculating about possible futures, they seem to enjoy reducing their worldview to an apocalyptic fantasy of not only their own demise but many others, dragging us along into another mass extinction."

Crocodile: "Swan, Dolphin, my watery comrades, good to see you here in Venice! Are you here to visit the Biennale as well? I swam straight from Jurassic Park because I

38 T.J. Demos, *Against the Anthropocene: Visual Culture and Environment* (Berlin: Sternberg Press, 2017).

39 Michael Marder, "The Coronavirus Is Us," *The New York Times* (3 March 2020), https://www.nytimes.com/2020/03/03/opinion/the-coronavirus-is-us.html.

wouldn't want to miss anything of this media spectacle."

"Confrère Crocodile, are you aware of the fact that the three of us are only present here in the Venice canals as figures of human make-believe, figments of their imagination?'

"Their projections do not make us less real, Swan!"

"Very Lacanian of you, to claim that we exist—not unlike God—because a collective of minds has projected us into becoming something mightily real. You are a true idealist, believing in the mind-dependency of matter."

"I beg to differ! Recently I spoke with my kinfolk the Black Caiman in the Amazon, and they presented me with an interesting analogy. When the Notre Dame in Paris was burning, the world's media covered every moment of it and billionaires rushed in to offer funding for its restoration. Right now the Amazon is burning. It has been burning for weeks now. No media coverage. No billionaires. My point is that today, for humans to feel empathic towards a certain cause, it has to be massively mediated for the matter to become a shared concern."

Swan: "For me your analogy is another Red Cardinal example of human exceptionalism and anthropocentrism: they salvage their history, their glorified past, but continue to be incapable of taking collective responsibility for, say, the 'lungs' of the Earth—not that I enjoy addressing the Earth through anthropomorphic qualities. A similar thing is happening now: We have become media emblems in a human feel-good story. The Earth isn't cleansing itself: that's eco-fascism dressed in New Age clothing.[40] We did not 'return' to the Venice canals; we were either already marginally present, or never there in the first place. The water of the canals is not cleaner, it just appears clearer. The self-pity is astounding: 'Kinda feeling like the Earth just sent us [humanity] to our rooms to think about what we've done.'"

Dolphin: "I did like this one: 'Climate Change needs to hire coronavirus's publicist.' You see, in line with Donna Haraway's thinking, facts travel with their apparatuses, but some truth-claims on facts travel badly, especially under today's predominant dissociative Trumpian logic of post-truth. Anything goes—'I dress my opinion with the apparatus of pseudoscience, and I can get away with it because most are not capable of thought in the first place.'[41] In this case, humanity tends to disassociate climate change from the alarming need for change and action, denying the connection that the coronavirus enjoys. The coronavirus is understood as acutely urgent because it can directly harm and endanger humanity's subsistence, whereas the ecological breakdown and climate regime are abstractions informing a type of 'mea culpa; it's not my fault.'"

Swan: "Philosopher Thomas Metzinger has an interesting take on that. He proposes that when humans act, their selves are 'translucent'—they act as an agent, but the sources of their agency are fundamentally invisible to them. At other times, the self is what he calls 'opaque,' meaning that humans have access to themselves in certain kinds of cases and ways as the (conscious) framers of the content of their experience.[42] They catch themselves in the act of thinking, unlike us animals, giving them the capacity to reflect on themselves and other selves, consciously experiencing another human being's movement as meaningful. However, when it comes to catching oneself in the act of thinking about one's self in relation to the ecological breakdown and non-human animals, this model seems to collapse into transparent 'business-as-usual' animality."

"As a Dolphin, I get sick of seeing myself in the shape of memes, and I think that is where the main problem of the disconnect lies: the fact that images are replacing and giving form to experience, that the images we currently have at our disposal don't allow the experiential feedback loop of humanity vis-à-vis the climate regime to come full circle. They may offer a bit of a breather, but writer and researcher Irmgard Emmelhainz makes this essential argument: 'This is cognitive capitalism deriving surplus value from the volume and velocity of images circulating: what is seen, said or shown is irrelevant, what matters is the sheer volume of content circulating around intensive global networks of communication. Within this vector, images acquire value and power by means of being seen; material things—say, the living environment—are no longer consumed directly, but operate instead as cognitive signs embedded in and around viewers. The acceleration and proliferation of cognitive signs is another feature of cognitive capitalism's subjugation—submitting the mind to an ever-increasing pace of perceptual stimuli. In this context, seeing means accelerating perception in the fields of everyday experience, or rather, the field of trivial visual analogies of experience: a kind of groundless, accelerated tautological vision derived from constant passive observation. When images and aesthetic experience—dissociated from human vision and directly tied to power and capital—have been turned into cognition and thus into empty sensations or tautological truths about reality, the image of the Anthropocene is still to come. In short, images of the Anthropocene are missing. It is first necessary to transcend our incapacity to imagine an alternative or something better by drawing a distinction between images and imagery. Although it is relayed by the optic nerve, the picture does not make an image. In order to make images, it is necessary to make vision assassinate perception; to ground vision, and then to perform—as in artistic activity—and think vision as a critical activity.'"[43]

Swan: "It's not very attractive to upload antiquated and irrelevant mental software, let alone produce it."

Crocodile: "As Ebola travelled by car and Corona travelled by airplane, so did we travel as imagery on the super-highway of the digital sphere; but how to overcome the social contagion of reductive and numbing viral imagery?"

Dolphin: "Fundamentally, humanity fails to perceive culture as nature. For me that has a lot to do with the absence of consciousness of a common interest. They are their own individual projects; surely *we* are not to blame for lacking consciousness here. Just as #socialdistancing is all the rage now, we are also suffering from a crisis of relationality, to invoke the words of Félix Guattari, a feigned proximity without intimacy. What we need is a refraction of vision to proffer images (and actions), imagining and treating nature as not only a rights-bearing subject, but a political subject."

40 Nick Estes (@nick_w_estes), "The earth isn't "cleansing itself,"" Twitter message, March 20, 2020, https://twitter.com/nick_w_estes/status/1241091924783595520?lang=en.

41 Donna Haraway, *Modest-Witness@Second-Millennium. FemaleMan-Meet-OncoMouse: Feminism and Technoscience* (New York: Routledge, 2018).

42 Heidi M. Ravven, *The Self Beyond Itself: An Alternative History of Ethics, the New Brain Sciences, and the Myth of Free Will* (New York: The New Press, 2013).

43 Irmgard Emmelhainz, "Images do Not Show: The Desire to See in the Antrhopocene," in *Art in the Anthropocene: Encounters Among Aesthetics, Politics, Environments and Epistomologies*, ed. H. Davis, E. Turpin (London: Open Humanities Press, 2015), 131–142.

Try to imagine the expression on your face "when an e-mail finds you well in these strange and uncertain times." It tends to find you in the "comfort" of the domestic sphere, except on the rare occasions when you leave to scavenge for food in the supermarket. Such domestic comfort is relative, that is, insofar as it provides ample space for your paranoia to flourish. "Perhaps the virus just flew through the open window? Is this containment a new exercise in statecraft?" While strolling outside you see phone-lit faces staring out of windows, taking snapshots of socially-distanced city life. You're reminded of the idea that romanticizing quarantine is a class privilege, but the thought quickly fades to the back of your mind when you notice that your favorite pasta brand is sold out (again)! You join the end of the line, expertly performing the fine art of one-point-five-meter queuing that you learned in the past month—quite the feat, considering you're not even British. You've grown so used to the ritual that a few moments pass before you notice that you are standing behind a line of deer, boars, goats, even monkeys. Yet you're not surprised in the slightest: nature has returned to the city. Animals are enjoying the relative stillness of city life, returning to squares, and now—without tourists around to feed them—even grocery shopping in supermarkets.

Your world feels increasingly like an unsettling combination of Orwell's *1984* in a light Ballardian broth of "wild" animals feasting on the corpses of domestic specimen, perhaps with a pinch of Jeff VanderMeer's *Annihilation*. "The virus is destroying everything. It's not destroying. It's making something new." Obviously, capitalism is culpable, but you wonder: how exactly does the socioeconomic sphere interface with the biological, and what insights might you gain from the experience of the pandemic? You may need to take a step back: the basic logic of capital expansion connects previously isolated or harmless viral strains to hyper-competitive environments. In other words (which came to you from China): "As capital accumulation subsumes new territories, animals will be pushed into less accessible areas where they will come into contact with previously isolated disease strains, all while these animals themselves are becoming targets for commodification as even the wildest subsistence species are being roped into agricultural value chains. Similarly, this expansion pushes humans closer to these animals and these environments, which may increase the interface (and spillover) between wild nonhuman populations and newly urbanized rurality. This gives the virus more opportunity and resources to mutate in a way that allows it to infect humans, pushing up the probability of biological spillover. The geography of industry itself is never quite so cleanly urban or rural anyways. Capitalism is already global, and already totalizing. It no longer has an edge or border with some natural, non-capitalist sphere beyond it, and there is therefore no great chain of development in which "backward" countries follow those ahead of them on their way up the value chain, nor any true wilderness capable of being preserved in some sort of pure, untouched condition. Instead, capital merely has a subordinated hinterland, itself fully subsumed within global value chains."[44]

You wonder what motivated all of these more or less wild animals to frequent, in increasing numbers, the urbanized environments that have been depopulated by humans during the corona pandemic. Surely these creatures did not all travel from the hinterland to the inner capital; they were never included in such vectors to begin with. But how to explain the deer populations now residing in parks, the mountain goats roaming the empty streets? Was their presence and proximity to humans previously ignored or barely tolerated, whereas now they are testing and pushing the boundaries between the natural and the cultural? (Now, that is, that their stomping grounds within cultivated natural reserves have been abandoned by humans?) And what about those interstitial urban species, like rats, pigeons and cockroaches—are *they* a byproduct of capitalism? Has the city become a new interzone where many species meet?

It has become your task—perhaps not for the first time, but now historicized before you in the shape of a mountain goat staring into your eyes—to sublate the distinction between the natural and the social, between nature and culture, in order to study the material environment in which this virus is manifesting. You also understand that the ecological breakdown wrought by lasting accumulation has extended both upward into the current planetary climate regime and downward into the microbiological substrata of life on Earth. But where to find a grounding, or at least a middle point from which to formulate a movement? How to balance the treatment of natural resources as "ecosystem services," with the sole purpose of gratifying humanity's needs, and the "ecology of disease" brought on by this treatment? To return to normality or business-as-usual—whatever that means to you—now seems undoable; normality was the problem, as the popular slogan goes. But how might capitalism look in the absence of progress—if ever—but especially when political systems are so deeply invested in necropolitical schemes exemplified by the statement, "Some of you must die for the U.S. economy to live."[45]

Nevertheless, the fragmentation and consistency of the discourse of individual responsibility as a governmental neoliberal policy (we are all victims of our compliance and complicity), alongside the unspecified temporal horizon of the coronavirus pandemic quarantine, establish a long-term dynamic of adaptation—one that may catalyze new forms of assembling and demands for socio-political transformation that recognize nature as a political subject. The escalation of the economic dimension and social contagion of the coronavirus pandemic reveals clear and painful linkages to the current climate regime; the worldwide existential rupture has been triggered by a microscopic pathogen incapable of having intent, that nevertheless urges humanity to think about different forms of symbiosis. Here, symbiosis is understood not as direct political alliance, but as a way of staying with the trouble and learning that we have never been individuals but instead holobionts that evolve together.[46] Or, in the words of Donna Haraway, "To be animal is to become-with bacteria, viruses and many other sorts of critters."[47] She explains: "The cultivation of viral response-abilities, carrying meanings and materials

44 Chuang, "Social Contagion: Microbiological Class War in China," Chuang (26 February 2020), http://chuangcn.org/2020/02/social-contagion/.

45 Jennifer Johnson, "We are not the virus," *Verso* (27 March 2020), https://www.versobooks.com/blogs/4622-we-are-not-the-virus.

46 *In 1991 Lynn Margulis proposed any physical association between individuals of different species for significant portions of their lifetime constitutes a 'symbiosis' and that all participants are bionts, such that the resulting association is a holobiont.* Donna Haraway, "Symbiogenesis, Sympoiesis, and Art Science Activisms for Staying with the Trouble," in *Arts of Living on a Damaged Planet*, ed. A. Tsing, H. Swanson, E. Gan, N. Bubandt (Minneapolis and London: University of Minnesota Press, 2017), 26; Lynn Margulis, "Symbiogenesis and Symbionticism," in *Symbiosis as a Source of Evolutionary Innovation: Speciation and Morphogenesis*, ed. L. Margulis and R. Fester (Boston: MIT Press, 1991), 1–14.

47 Haraway, *Staying with the Trouble*, 65.

across kinds in order to infect processes and practices that might yet ignite epidemics of multi species recuperation and maybe even flourishing on terra in ordinary times and places."[48]

We have come to recognize that the transmission of the virus, beyond the strictly biological, is social and ethical, and that the social realm of humanity will have to facilitate a war on the structures of society itself in order to establish an equal footing with all that matters beyond humanity. These "response-abilities" may well involve formulating an ethics of withdrawal, taking legal actions to demand that corporations and governments "physically distance" from monocultural livestock and extractivist practices, evolving fossil-burning man by learning how to not exhaust natural resources from other nonhuman-animals. We must not judge or blame animals for the potential risks they inflict on humans through zoonosis, but rather acknowledge a metaphorical but radically devastating anthroponosis in ourselves (you know who you are).

Whereas hand sanitizer fails to distinguish between harmful and useful bacteria, some parts of humanity fail to unify nature and culture as *naturecultures*, which in this context acknowledges that human, animal, and ecological health are inextricably linked and need to be studied and treated holistically. In light of the conditions fostering viral outbreaks, this pandemic should be considered, in the words of philosopher Bruno Latour, as a "dress rehearsal."[49] A return to business-as-usual and a recuperation of lost production will trigger additional crises of capitalism in seemingly non-economic guises such as more pandemics, famine, flooding, sea-level rises, ocean and soil acidification, further degradation of biodiversity, and the ongoing depletion of life forms. In that sense, according to philosopher Andreas Philippopoulos-Mihalopoulos, the coronavirus demands of us a quintessentially Spinozan ethics of positioning, of placing one's body in a geography of awareness of the effects circulating between us and others. At any one moment, we carry with us our whole lives and deaths, and we converge with other bodies, human and nonhuman, forming temporary or more enduring assemblages. We are all collective bodies leading collective lives with other collective bodies.[50] Nature is not only a passive material reservoir and support structure for human activity, but an assembler, one that links the living and the inert (while being both), that forms a basis to reveal the social and material, beyond the realm of the formal, which leads us back to being animals…

48 Haraway, *Staying with the Trouble*, 114.
49 Bruno Latour, "Is This a Dress-Rehearsal?," Critical Enquiry (26 March 2020), https://critinq.wordpress.com/2020/03/26/is-this-a-dress-rehearsal/.
50 Andreas Philippopoulos-Mihalopoulos, "Covid: The Ethical Disease," Critical Legal Thinking (13 March 2020), https://criticallegalthinking.com/2020/03/13/covid-the-ethical-disease/?fbclid=IwAR1tnPGLC38L35BquiHHSEf9g3z20pypcvRp2q_kUIEKaArjyxxY8_wgd4M.

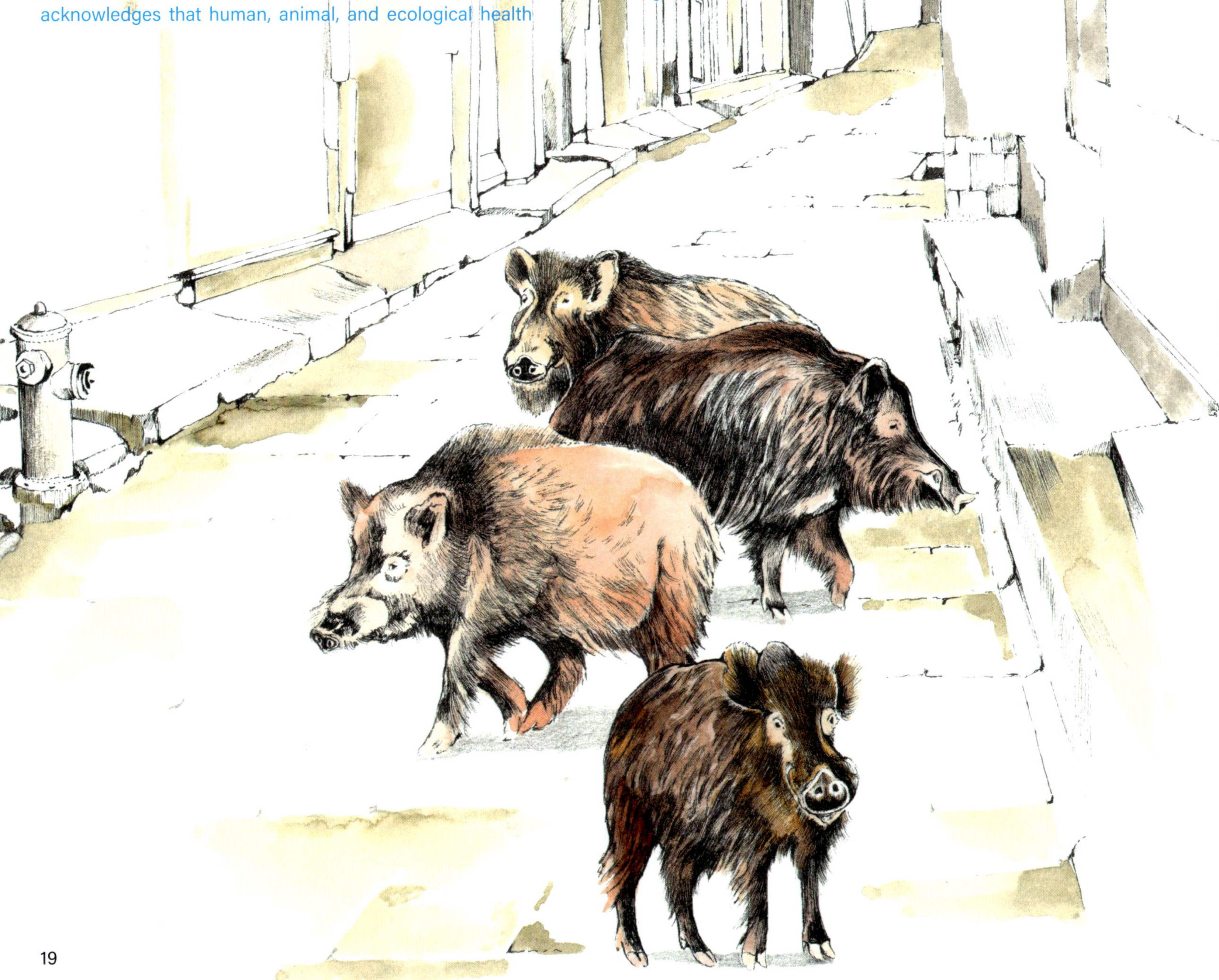

CORONA ANIMAL SPOTTING INVENTORY

DATE:	SPECIES:	LOCATION:	ACTION:
IN THE WILD			
11 March 2020	ELEPHANTS	Yunnan, China	Intoxication, Sleeping
12 March 2020	MONKEYS	Lopburi, Thailand	Brawling (Food war)
17 March 2020	DOLPHINS	Venice, Italy	Returning, appearing
18 March 2020	SWANS	Venice, Italy	Appearing, Returning
18 March 2020	HUMPBACK WHALE	Venice, Italy	Unknown
19 March 2020	CROCODILE	Venice, Italy	Frolicking
19 March 2020	DEER	Zakopane, Poland	Wandering
19 March 2020	WHITE RHINOS	New York, US	Flooding city
19 March 2020	WILD BOARS	Barcelona, Spain	Descending
24 March 2020	COUGARS	Santiago, Chile	Visiting, Wandering
25 March 2020	SEAGULLS, PELICANS	Coast of Lima, Peru	Taking over
26 March 2020	CIVET CAT	Meppayur, India	Roaming
26 March 2020	INDIAN BISON	Karnataka, India	Strolling
27 March 2020	COYOTES	San Francisco, US	Roaming, Wandering
27 March 2020	NILGAI	Noida, India	Walking freely
28 March 2020	KILLER WHALES	Vancouver, Canada	Being spotted
29 March 2020	SEA TURTLES	Coast of Odisha, India	Nesting
30 March 2020	WILD BOARS	Bergamo, Italy	Returning
31 March 2020	CORONA HORSE	Andhra Pradesh, India	Spreading awareness
31 March 2020	KASHMIRI GOATS	Llandudno, Wales, UK	Taking over
2 April 2020	PEACOCKS	Mumbai, India	Dancing
3 April 2020	DEER	London, UK	Resting
5 April 2020	ALLIGATORS	Myrtle Beach, US	Reclaiming, Strolling
6 April 2020	SHEEP	Monmouthshire, Wales, UK	Playing (Roundabout)
7 April 2020	RHINO	Chitwan, Nepal	Chasing man
8 April 2020	MONKEYS	Ahmedabad, India	Scrambling for food
13 April 2020	ZEBRA	Paris, France	Escaping zoo
13 April 2020	DEER	Paris, France	Wandering
13 April 2020	MONKEYS	Mumbai, India	Pool party
15 April 2020	WILD BOARS	Haifa, Israel	Taking over
20 April 2020	KANGAROO	Adelaide, Australia	Hopping
21 April 2020	JELLYFISH	Venice, Italy	Swimming
21 April 2020	SHEEP	Ebbw Vale, Wales, UK	Visiting McDonalds
23 April 2020	FOX CUBS	Toronto, Canada	Going for a walk
26 April 2020	DOLPHINS	Istanbul, Turkey	Exploring the Bosphorus
Date Unknown	HIPPOPOTAMUS	Brussels, Belgium	Unknown
Date Unknown	RACCOON	Location unknown	Visiting library
IN CAPTIVITY			
17 March 2020	PENGUINS	Shedd Aquarium, Chicago, US	Enjoying a guided tour
5 April 2020	TIGERS	Bronx Zoo, New York, US	Testing positive
6 April 2020	PANDAS	Ocean Park, Hong Kong	Having sex

Bestiary of Corona Animals
by Niekolaas Johannes Lekkerkerk

Onomatopee Z0027
ISBN 978-94-93148-31-4
First edition of 500 copies

Published by

Onomatopee
Lucas Gasselstraat 2A
5613 LB Eindhoven
The Netherlands

Edited by Tamar Shafrir
Graphic design by Sabo Day
Illustrations by Lisa Rampilli
Proofreading and research assistance by Sergi Pera Rusca
Text by Niekolaas Johannes Lekkerkerk
Printed by robstolk®, Amsterdam

Acknowledgements

Thank you to all the animal correspondents and respondents. Thank you to Sabo Day, Lisa Rampilli, Sergi Pera Rusca, and Tamar Shafrir for the collaboration. Thank you to Kelly-ann van Steveninck for refreshing and sharpening my mind. Thank you to Robert Lekkerkerk and Sanny Kastelein for supporting this publication. Thank you to Merel Bem for keeping an exhaustive list of corona animals. Thank you to Nina Swaep for the second opinion.